The Psalms of Ascent and Their Prophetic Significance for the 2020s and 2030s

by

Kathryn Sitterle

Psalms of Ascent and Their Prophetic Significance for the 2020s and 2030s

Copyright © 2025 by Kathryn Sitterle

ALL RIGHTS RESERVED

No part of this book may be reproduced or transmitted in any form or by any means, electronic or mechanical, including photocopying, recording, or by any information retrieval system.

The picture on this cover is from Grace Community Church located in Glen Rose, Texas, and permission to share it was granted by Rick Stone, head of the Education/Administration staff.

The DVD "Psalms of Ascent" with Dr. Jeffrey Seif, Sandra Levitt, and others from Zola Levitt Ministries, Inc. demonstrates how timely these psalms are for believers today, and permission was granted to share their comments on these Psalms of Ascent.

Unless otherwise noted, all Bible references are taken from the *One New Man Bible: Revealing Jewish Roots and Power*, copyright © 2011 by William J. Morford, published by True Potential, Inc., Traveler's Rest, South Carolina. References marked "NKJV" are from *The Holy Bible, New King James Version*, copyright © 1979, 1980, 1982, 1990 by Thomas Nelson, Inc., Nashville, Tennessee. References marked "NCV" are from *The Holy Bible, New Century Version*®, copyright © 1987, 1988, 1991 by Thomas Nelson, Inc. All rights reserved. Used by permission.

Published By:

Amoq (Hebrew Roots)
www.ThePublishedWord.com

ISBN: 978-1-964665-29-0

Printed on Demand in the U.S., the U.K., Australia, and the UAE
For worldwide distribution

Dedication: To the Yeshua/Jesus
Who is the True Vine

Without You, this, my second book, would not have been possible. You are my All, and I love You with all my heart.

The Aaronic Priestly Blessing
(Numbers 6:24-27)

The LORD will bless you and He will keep you.

The LORD will make His face to shine upon you and He will be gracious to you.

The LORD will lift His countenance to you and He will establish Shalom for you.

And they will put My name upon the children of Israel and I will bless them.

Contents

Introduction .... Page 6

Psalm 120 .... Page 9
Psalm 121 .... Page 10
Psalm 122 .... Page 11
Psalm 123 .... Page 12
Psalm 124 .... Page 13
Psalm 125 .... Page 14
Psalm 126 .... Page 15
Psalm 127 .... Page 16
Psalm 128 .... Page 17
Psalm 129 .... Page 18
Psalm 130 .... Page 19
Psalm 131 .... Page 20
Psalm 132 .... Page 21
Psalm 133 .... Page 23
Psalm 134 .... Page 24
Psalm 135 .... Page 25
Psalm 136 .... Page 27
Psalm 137 .... Page 30
Psalm 138 .... Page 31

Introduction

The book, *Hidden Prophecies in the Psalms,*[1] written by the late great prophecy teacher, J. R. Church, really got me hooked on the Book of Psalms being relevant for revelation and prophecy for the 1900s and beyond to the soon coming of our LORD, Jesus the Christ. When I went to Israel for the first time in 2010, I saw somewhere written that Psalm 120, which is the beginning of the Psalms of Ascent, had revelation for the year 2011, and that year began the Arab Spring, an uprising in Arab countries, starting in Tunisia, going into Libya and Egypt, and struggling to go into other Muslim countries. Then the pattern continued to Psalm 121 for the year 2012. I did not see what Psalm was the last in this series.

I had heard from prophecy teachers that the seven books between the book of Hebrews and the book of Revelation referred to a seven-year period that starts with the book of James telling the rich that they will weep and can start another seven-year *Smetah* cycle in which the rich will weep, such as what happened in 2001 with the dot.com bubble, and again with the year 2008 that saw the mortgage crisis. Psalms 120 to 134, known as the "Psalms of Ascent" or "Song of Ascent" were associated with Israel's Pilgrim Feasts when pilgrims from far and wide went up to Jerusalem to worship in the Temple.

1. Oklahoma City, Oklahoma (Prophecy Publications: 1986)

But just as has been written

"What eye did not see and ear did not hear and did not go up upon the heart of man, what God prepared for those who love Him."

But God has revealed them to us through the Spirit, for the Spirit searches all things, even the deep things of God.

1 Corinthians 2:9-10

The Psalms of Ascent and Their Prophetic Significance for the 2020s and 2030s

Now it shall come to pass in the latter days

That the mountain of the Lord's House

Shall be established on the top of the mountains

And shall be exalted above the hills;

And all nations shall flow to it.

      Isaiah 2:2, NKJV

According to the Book of Psalms in many Bibles and to Jewish tradition, Psalms 120 to 134 are known as the Psalms of Ascent or simply the Song of Ascent. These psalms were sung by pilgrims going up the mountain to worship in the Temple in Jerusalem during the three mandatory feasts, which are Passover, Pentecost (Shavuot), and Tabernacles (or Succoth). The DVD "Psalms of Ascent" with Dr. Jeffrey Seif, Sandra Levitt, and others from Zola Levitt Ministries, Inc. demonstrates how timely these Psalms are for believers in Father God and His Son, Jesus (Yeshua in Hebrew/Aramaic) today.

The Three Feasts Mandatory Each Year

(Deuteronomy 16:16)

Three times in a year all your males will appear before the LORD your God in the place which He will choose during the Feast of Unleavened Bread, in the Feast of Weeks [Pentecost], and in the Feast of Sukkot. And they will not appear before the LORD empty. Each man will give as he is able, according to the blessing of the LORD your God which He has given you.

Pastor James Durham, a friend of mine since 2010 when I went to Israel for the first time, served in the U.S. Army almost thirty years as an active chaplain and retired at the rank of Colonel (5-star I might add). He was a pastor and church planter before and after he retired. During one conversation I had with him, he explained that there is a spiritual end and also a physical end of many things. Concerning the Psalms of Ascent, he mentioned that Psalms 135 to 138 are also part of the Psalms of Ascent, and they add the physical end to these psalms or Divine completion.

In the following pages, after each Psalm that is written, the first comment will be from the Psalms of Ascent DVD from Psalm 120 to 134. Then I will make a comment from my personal analysis. I believe Psalm 120 can correlate to the year 2020 and Psalm 121 to the year 2021, continuing the pattern to the year 2034 for Psalm 134.

Psalms 120-134 "The Psalms of Ascent"

Psalm 120

In my distress I cried to the LORD and He heard me.

Deliver my being, LORD, from lying lips, from a deceitful tongue.

What will the deceitful tongue give to you? Or what will it add to you?

Sharp arrows of the mighty, with coals of a broom brush.

Woe is me, that I sojourn in Meshekh, that I dwell in the tents of Kedar.

[Meshekh was the second son of Ismael, son of Abraham and Hagar.]

My body has long dwelt with someone who hates peace.

I am for peace, but when I speak, they are for war.

Comments

"The Tents of Kedar" refers to Bedouins and the Meshekh information comes from a Zola Levitt Presents TV show and also their DVD on the Psalms of Ascent. Bedouins are nomadic Arab tribes that have historically inhabited the desert regions in the Arabian Peninsula, Mesopotamia, Africa, and Israel.

Joe Biden became acting President in the year 2020. Could he and/or someone in his administration have been for war? Or could this refer to representatives in the United Nations?

A juniper tree is considered by many to be the broom brush that the Bible references, whose main use happens to be as a broom, hence its name.

Psalm 121

I shall lift up my eyes unto the hills: from where will my help come?

My help comes from the LORD, Who made heaven and earth.

He will <u>not</u> allow your foot to be moved. He Who keeps you will <u>not</u> slumber.

Behold, He that keeps Israel will neither slumber nor sleep.

The LORD is your keeper. The LORD is your shade upon your right hand.

The sun will not strike you by day, nor the moon by night,

The LORD will preserve you from all chaos, He will preserve your eternal life.

The LORD will guard your going out and your coming in from this time forth and even for evermore.

Comments:

This is the "Traveler's Psalm," say those on "The Psalms of Ascent" DVD.

I can see why this is called the "Travelers Psalm" because of all of the vocabulary related to travel in a hilly area unfriendly to travelers. This Psalm reminds those of you who are traveling that the LORD, Who made the Heaven and the Earth, will <u>not</u> allow your foot to be moved, and He will keep you from all chaos. He will preserve your eternal life and guard your going out and your coming in.

Psalm 122

I was glad when they said to me, Let us go into the House of the LORD.

Our feet have stood within your gates, O Jerusalem.

Jerusalem is built as a city that is compact together: wherever the tribes go up, the tribes of Yah, to the testimony of Israel, to give thanks to the name of the LORD.

For there are set thrones of judgment, the thrones of the house of David.

Pray fervently for the Shalom of Jerusalem! They that love you will have security.

Peace be within your walls, security within your palaces.

For my brothers' and companions' sake, I shall now say, Peace be within you.

Because of the House of the Lord our God I shall seek your good.

Comments

The House of the Lord and the House of David are significant references back to the time of King Solomon who built the Temple or House of God I Jerusalem.

On October 7, 2023, Israel was attacked by Hamas. This Psalm 122 for 2022 reminded the Israelis that God had thrones of Judgment and to pray <u>feverently for the Shalom (Peace) of Israel)</u> for what was coming in 2023.

Psalm 123

Unto you do I lift up my eyes, O You Who lives in the heavens.

Behold, as the eyes of servants look to the hand of their masters, as the eyes of a maiden to the hand of her mistress, so our eyes are upon the LORD our God, until He is gracious to us.

Be gracious to us, LORD, be gracious to us! For we are exceedingly filled with contempt.

Our life is exceedingly filled with the scorning of those who are at ease, with the contempt of the proud.

Comments

Just as servants depend on their masters, the people of Israel are to depend on God.

On October 7, 2023, Hamas and several other Palestinian militant groups launched coordinated armed attacks from the Gaza Strip into southern Israel, the first invasion of Israeli territory since the 1948 Arab-Israeli War.

Psalm 124

If it had not been the LORD Who was on our side, now may Israel say,

If it had not been the LORD Who was on our side when men rose up against us,

then they would have swallowed us up alive when their wrath was kindled against us:

then the waters would have overwhelmed us, the stream would have gone over our body:

then the deliberately wicked waters would have gone over our body.

Blessed be the LORD, Who has given us as a prey to their teeth.

Our life has escaped like a bird out of the snare of the fowlers: the snare is broken and we have escaped.

Our help is in the name of the LORD, Who made heaven and earth.

Comments

The Hebrew letter MEM is symbolized by water, which refers usually to troubled water. The 1948 Arab-Israeli conflict erupted as Israel was again becoming a nation. Then Israel also had major conflicts in the Six-Day War and in 1973 the Yom Kippur War.

However, Psalm 124 seems to be describing Hamas attacking Israel on the last day of the Festival of Sukkot, which was a Sabbath Day, October 7, 2023.

Psalm 125

Those who trust in the LORD will be like Mount Zion, which cannot be removed, but abides forever.

As the mountains are round about Jerusalem, so the LORD is round about His people, from now and forevermore.

For the rod of the wicked will not rest upon the lot of the righteous, lest the righteous put forth their hands for injustice.

Do good, LORD, to those who are good and to those who are upright in their hears.

As for such as turn aside to their crooked ways, the LORD will lead them forth with workers of wickedness, but peace will be upon Israel.

Comments

God's abiding love surrounds His people like the mountains circle Jerusalem.

God's people in the U.S., Europe, and other places in the world will be strong during tribulation; they will not be moved. We also sense that Israel will go through challenges that will lead to turmoil for her, but the LORD says that peace will be upon this hallowed land.

Psalm 126

When the LORD turned back the captivity of Zion, we were like those who dream.

Then our mouth was filled with laughter and our tongue with singing: then they said among the nations, The LORD has done great things for them.

The LORD has done great things for us, for which we are glad.

Turn back our captivity, LORD, as the streams in the Negev.

Those who sow in tears will reap in joy.

He who goes forth and weeps, scattering the seed, will doubtless come back with rejoicing, bringing his sheaves.

Comments

You will persevere during hard times; you will even be able to laugh during those hard times.

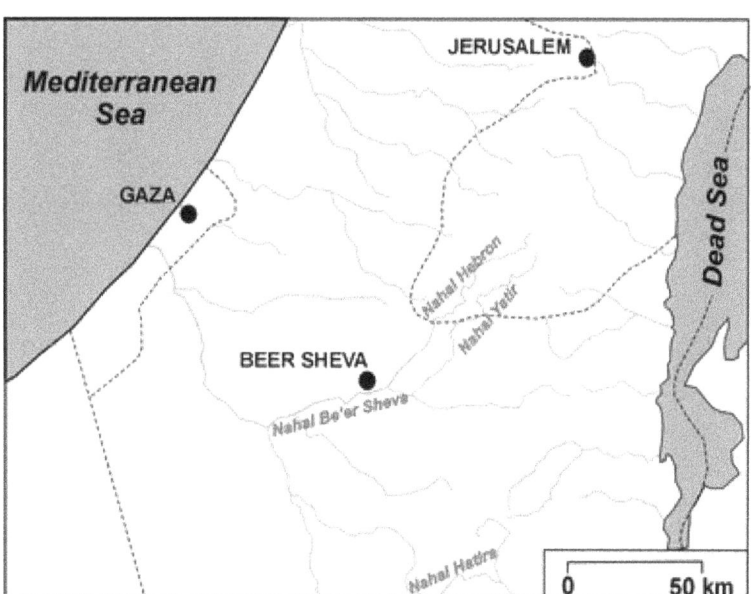

Instead of a comment, I have provided this map of the Negev Desert in Israel.

Psalm 127

Unless the LORD builds the house, those who build it labor in vain: unless the LORD guards the city, the watchman wakes in vain.

It is vain for you to rise up early, to sit up late, to eat the bread of toils, for so He gives His beloved in sleep;

Lo, children are a heritage of the LORD: the fruit of the womb is a reward.

As arrows are in the hand of a mighty man, so are children of your youth.

Happy is the man who has his quiver full of them. They will not be ashamed, but they will speak with the enemies in the gate.

Comments

The introduction of this Psalm says it is for Solomon, who built the Temple for the Lord in Jerusalem. The LORD needs to build the house or they that build it labor in vain. People may sing this song and enjoy each other's company together corporately. And *"the fruit of the womb is a reward"* from the LORD.

In 2027, it may be that the LORD is preparing His people to rebuild the Temple in Jerusalem.

Psalm 128

Blessed is everyone who reveres the LORD, who walks in His Ways.

For you will eat the labor of your hands: happy will you be, and it will be well with you.

Your wife will be like a fruitful vine by the sides of your house: your children like olive plants all around your table.

Behold, that thus will the man be blessed who reveres the LORD.

The LORD will bless you from out of Zion, and you will see the good of Jerusalem all the days of your life.

And you will see your children's children, peace upon Israel.

Comments

This is a Psalm for the family. It addresses a godly family and the blessings a husband receives from his wife and children.

You will see your grandchildren when you revere the LORD and walk in His ways. You will eat well by the labor of your hands, and it will be well with you.

Psalm 129

Many a time have they afflicted me from my youth. Israel will now say, Many a time have they afflicted me from my youth, yet they have not prevailed against me.

The plowers plowed upon my back: they made their burrows long.

The LORD is righteous. He has cut asunder the cords of the wicked.

All those who hate Zion will be shamed and turned back.

They will be like the grass on the housetops, which withers before it grows up, with which the mower does not fill his hand, nor does he who binds sheaves fill his bosom.

Nor do those who go by say, The blessing of the LORD is upon you. We bless you in the name of the LORD.

Comments

God's people have been afflicted by bullies, but God has cut asunder the cords of the wicked.

They will run to and fro in the city. They will run on the wall, they will climb up on the houses, they will enter in at the windows like a thief. Joel 2:9

Psalm 130

Out of the depts have I cried to You, LORD.

Adonai [Lord], listen to my voice. Let your ears be attentive to the sound of my supplications [asking or begging for something].

If You, Yah [God], should take count of iniquities, my LORD, who will stand?

But there is forgiveness with You, so You will be revered.

I wait for the LORD. My body waits and I hope in His word.

My being waits for the LORD more than those who watch for the morning: I say, more than those who watch for the morning.

Let Israel hope in the LORD, for with the LORD there is loving kindness, and plenteous redemption is with Him.

And He will redeem Israel from all its iniquities.

Comments

I wait for the LORD. Let Israel hope in the LORD, for redemption is with Him.

Psalm 130 served for the year 2021 in which we were under COVID restrictions, and so many of us were "waiting on the Lord." Psalm 120 served for the year 2011, continuing the pattern to Psalm 138 for the year 2029.

Psalm 131

LORD, my heart is not haughty, nor my eyes lofty: neither do I exercise myself in great matters, or in things too wonderful for me.

Surely, I have calmed and quieted myself, like a child weaned of his mother: my very being is like a weaned child.

Isreal, yearn for the LORD, from now and forevermore!

Comments

God is represented here as a mother. A child is weaned from its mother's breasts after the baby is old enough to eat solid foods.

Continuing with the pattern mentioned in Psalm 130, then Psalm 131 would point to the year 2022, which actually was a word for the Israelis to keep in their heart. They would need it for the coming year 2023 … particularly when, on October 7, 2023, Hamas and several other militant groups launched coordinated armed attacks from the Gaza strip into southern Israel. As noted, it was the first invasion of Israeli territory since the 1938 Arab-Israeli War.

Psalm 132

LORD, remember David, all his afflictions, how he swore to the LORD, vowed to the Mighty God of Jacob.

Surely I shall not come into the tent of my house, or go up to my bed.

I shall not give sleep to my eyes, slumber to my eyelids,

until I find out a place for the LORD, a dwelling place for the Mighty One of Jacob.

Behold we heard of it at Ephratah: we found it in the fields of the wood.

We will go into His dwelling places: we will worship at His footstool.

Arise LORD, into you're your rest, You and the Ark of Your strength.

Your priests will be clothed with righteousness, and Your pious pious ones will shout for joy.

For Your servant David's sake do not turn away the face of Your anointed.

The LORD has sworn in truth to David; He will not turn from it, from the fruit of your body I will set upon your throne.

If your children will keep My covenant and My testimony that I shall teach them, their children will also sit upon your throne forevermore.

For the Lord has chosen Zion; He has desired it for His habitation.

This is My rest forever: I shall dwell here, for I have desired it.

I shall abundantly bless its provision. I shall satisfy its poor with bread.

Psalm 132 continued

I shall also clothe its priests with salvation, and its pious ones will shout aloud for joy.

There I shall make the horn of David to bud: I have ordained a lamp for My anointed.

I shall clothe his enemies with shame, but upon himself will his crown glitter.

Comments

The following two verses were chosen to sum up this Psalm 132:

I shall not give sleep to my eyes, slumber to my eyelids, until I find out a place for the LORD, a dwelling place for the Mighty One of Jacob.

For the LORD has chosen Zion: He has desired it for His habitation.

This is my rest forever: I shall dwell here, for I have desired it.

Continuing the pattern of Psalm 132 for the year 2023, you will notice this Psalm is the longest of all of the Psalms of Ascent, and the special significance this Psalm has for the Israelis, who have experienced Hamas and several other militant groups that launched coordinated armed attacks from the Gaza strip into southern Israel. The Lord chose Zion in Israel for His dwelling place to dwell forever.

Psalm 133

Behold, how good and how pleasant it is for brothers to dwell together in unity.

It is like the precious ointment upon the head, that ran down upon the beard, Aaron's beard: that went down over the collar of his garments, like the dew of Hermon, that descended upon the mountains of Zion, for there the LORD commanded the blessing, Life forevermore!

Comments

The following two verses were chosen to sum up this Psalm 133:

Behold, how good and how pleasant it is for brothers to dwell together in unity.

Precious ointment upon the head, that ran down upon the beard, Aaron's beard: that went down over the collar of his garments, like the dew of Hermon. [Mt. Hermon in northern Israel]

Before the events of October 7, 2023, Jews living in Israel were growing more and more divided politically and religiously. Now after October 7, 2023, Israelis have become closer to one another as they have a common enemy they must fight for survival and for living a joy-filled life.

Psalm 134 is the End of the Psalms of Ascent

Behold bless the LORD, all you servants of the LORD, who stand by night in the House of the LORD.

Life up your hands in the Sanctuary! Bless the LORD!

The LORD Who made heaven and earth will bless you from Zion.

Comments

The following two verses were chosen to sum up this Psalm 134:

Behold bless the LORD, all you servants of the LORD, who stand by night in the House of the LORD.

Life up your hands in the Sanctuary! Bless the LORD!

John 2:19 and 2:21

Y'shua answered and said to them, "You must destroy this Sanctuary [Temple] and in three days I shall raise it." But He was talking about the Sanctuary of His body.

1 Corinthians 6:19, NCV

You should know that your body is a temple for the Holy Spirit who is in you. You have received the Holy Spirit from God.

Isaiah 2:3, NKJV

Many people shall come and say, "Come, and let us go up to the mountain of the LORD, to the house of the God of Jacob; He will teach us His ways, and we shall walk in His paths." For out of Zion shall go forth the Law, and the Word of the LORD from Jerusalem.

Psalms 135 to 138

As noted earlier, my friend, Pastor James Durham, whom I met on my first trip to Israel in 2010, mentioned that there is a physical end and also a spiritual end of many things pertaining to God's creation. He told me that the "Psalms of Ascent" continue to Psalm 138. Psalm 138 would have influences on the years 2029 and also 2038. Pastor James has served in the ministry for more than forty-eight years. Thiry years were spent as an active-duty army Chaplain. In 2010, Pastor James retired from the military with the rank of Colonel. He is the author of several books that are relevant to today and to the days to come.

Psalm 135

HalleluYah! Praise the name of the LORD! Praise, you servants of the LORD.

You who stand in the House of the LORD, in the courts of the House of our God.

HalleluYah! For the LORD is good! Sing praises to His name, for it is Pleasant!

For Yah has chosen Jacob for Himself, Israel for His special treasure.

For I know that the LORD is great and our LORD is above all gods.

Whatever the LORD pleased, that He did in heaven and in earth, in the seas, and all deep places.

He causes the vapors to ascend from the ends of the earth. He makes lightnings for the rain. He brings the wind out of His treasuries.

Who smote the firstborn of Egypt, both of man and beast.

Who sent signs and wonders into your midst, O Egypt, upon Pharaoh and upon all his servants.

Psalm 135 Continued

Who smote great nations and slew mighty kings; Sihon king of the Amorite and Og king of Bashan and all the kingdoms of Canaan, and gave their land for a heritage, a heritage for Israel His people.

Your name, LORD, endures forever, Your memorial, LORD, throughout all generations.

For the LORD will judge His people and He Himself will have compassion concerning His servants.

The idols of the nations are silver and gold, the work of men's hands.

They have mouths, but they do not speak; they have eyes, but they do not see, they have ears, but they do not hear; neither is there any breath in their mouths. Those who make them will be like them: everyone who trusts in them.

House of Israel, Bless the LORD! House of Aaron, Bless the LORD!

House of Levi, Bless the LORD! You who revere the LORD, Bless the LORD! Blessed be the LORD out of Zion Who dwells at Jerusalem. HalleluYah!

My Comments

"**For I know that the LORD is great and our LORD is above all gods**" **(Verse 5). UFO or UAP disclosures must have happened or will happen in 2026, and there is also a message in this Psalm for the year 2035** "**in the Courts of the house of our God**" **(end of verse 2). If you want to know more about the Courts of Heaven, Robert Henderson is the author of several good books on this subject. These books are a wonderful place to receive information and revelation on what has been going on for some time in God's Courts in Heaven and with many of His people.**

Psalm 136

O give thanks to the LORD! For He is good, for His loving kindness endures forever.

O give thanks to the God of gods! For His loving kindness endures forever.

O give thanks to the Lord of lords! For His loving kindness endures forever.

To Him Who alone does great wonders, for His loving kindness endures forever.

To Him Who by wisdom made the heavens, for His loving kindness endures forever.

To Him Who stretched out the earth above the waters, for His loving kindness endures forever.

To Him Who made great lights, for His loving kindness endures forever.

The sun to rule by day, for His loving kindness endures forever.

The moon and stars to rule by night, for His loving kindness endures forever.

To Him Who smote Egypt in their firstborn, for His loving kindness endures forever:

And brought Israel out from among them, for His loving kindness endures forever.

With a strong hand and with an outstretched arm, for His loving kindness endures forever.

To Him Who divided the Red Sea in parts, for His loving kindness endures forever.

Psalm 136 continued

And made Israel to pass through the midst of it, for His loving kindness endures forever.

But overthrew Pharaoh and his army in the Sea of Reeds, for His loving kindness endures forever.

To Him Who led his people through the wilderness, for His loving kindness endures forever.

To Him Who smote great kings, for His loving kindness endures forever.

And slew famous kings, for His loving kindness endures forever.

Sihon king of the Amorites, for His loving kindness endures forever.

And Og the king of Bashan, for His loving kindness endures forever.

And gave their land for a heritage, for His loving kindness endures forever.

A heritage for Israel His servant, for His loving kindness endures forever.

Who remembered us in our low estate, for His loving kindness endures forever.

And has redeemed us from our enemies, for His loving kindness endures forever.

Who gives food to all flesh, for His loving kindness endures forever.

O give thanks to the God of Heaven, for His loving kindness endures forever.

My Comments on Psalm 136

"O give thanks to the God of gods! For His loving kindness endures forever." Again, this Psalm mentions gods, so disclosure of the alien gods may have happened or is going to happen, but do *NOT* forget His lovingkindness endures forever and ALL the things He has done for us since the beginning of time. This can be a message for **2027** and also a message for the year **2036**. Thank You, God. Praise You!

Psalm 137

By the rivers of Babylon, there we sat down; yes, we wept when we remembered Zion.

We hung our harps upon the willows in its midst.

For there those who carried us away captive required a song of us, and those who oppressed us required of us mirth [amusement, usually laughter] saying, "Sing us one of the songs of Zion."

How will we sing the LORD's song in a strange land?

If I forget you, O Jerusalem, my right hand will forget its skill.

If I do not remember you, my tongue will cleave to the roof of my mouth, if I do not prefer Jerusalem above my chief joy.

Remember, LORD, the children of Edom in the day of Jerusalem, who said, Raze it. Raze it to its foundation!

O daughter of Babylon, who is to be destroyed, happy will he be who repays you as you have served us.

Happy will he be who takes and dashes your little ones against the rock.

My Comments

The horrible deed done in this last line has often been perpetrated against Israel, even in the 21st century, especially by terrorists. Some of Jerusalem or parts of Israel may be going into captivity near the end of the age before their Messiah comes. This can be a message for 2028 and also a message for the year 2037.

Psalm 138

I shall praise You with my whole heart. Before the gods I shall sing praise to You.

I shall worship toward your holy Temple and praise Your name for Your loving kindness and for Your truth, for You have magnified Your word even above Your name.

In the day when I cried, You answered me, emboldened me with strength in my body.

All the kings of the earth will praise You, LORD, when they hear the words of Your mouth.

And they will sing in the Ways of the LORD, for great is the glory of the LORD.

Though the LORD is high, yet He has respect for the lowly; but the proud He knows from afar.

Though I walk in the midst of trouble, You will revive me. You will stretch forth Your hand against the wrath of my enemies and Your right hand will save me.

The LORD will perfect that which concerns me. Your loving kindness, LORD, endures forever. Do not forsake the works of Your own hands!

My Comments

"I shall praise You with my whole heart. Before the gods I shall sing praise to You." Three of these last four Psalms mention gods. So, there must be talk and or disclosure that has taken place about them. Do not forget to praise God with your whole heart. This can be a message for **2029**, and also there may be a message for the year **2038**.

www.ingramcontent.com/pod-product-compliance
Lightning Source LLC
Chambersburg PA
CBHW041638040426
42449CB00022B/3494